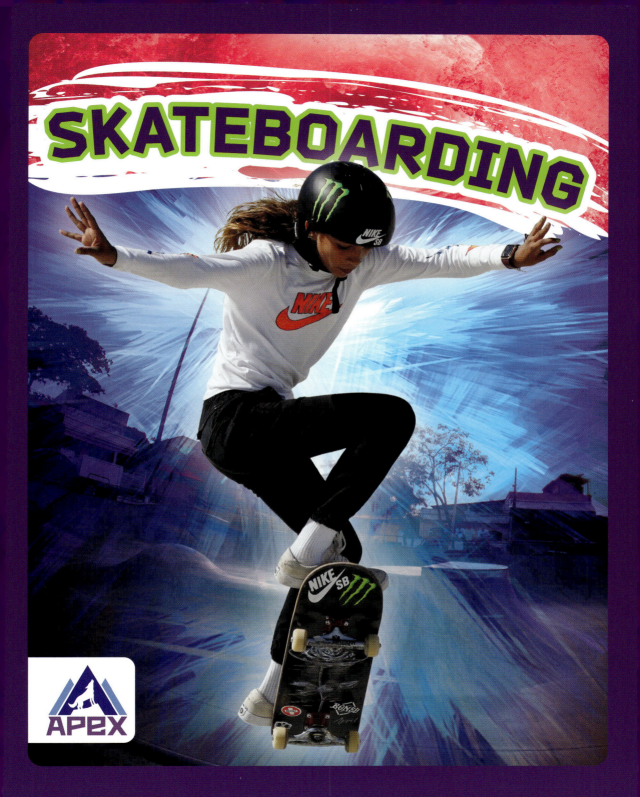

SKATEBOARDING

BY BETTIE BOSWELL

WWW.APEXEDITIONS.COM

Copyright © 2022 by Apex Editions, Mendota Heights, MN 55120. All rights reserved. No part of this book may be reproduced or utilized in any form or by any means without written permission from the publisher.

Apex is distributed by North Star Editions:
sales@northstareditions.com | 888-417-0195

Produced for Apex by Red Line Editorial.

Photographs ©: Alessandra Tarantino/AP Images, cover (skater), 1 (skater); Pexels, cover (background), 1 (background); Shutterstock Images, 4–5, 6–7, 8, 9, 13, 15, 20–21, 22–23, 25; iStockphoto, 10–11, 12, 16–17, 18, 19, 24, 27, 29; Ben Curtis/AP Images, 26

Library of Congress Control Number: 2021915734

ISBN
978-1-63738-154-0 (hardcover)
978-1-63738-190-8 (paperback)
978-1-63738-260-8 (ebook pdf)
978-1-63738-226-4 (hosted ebook)

Printed in the United States of America
Mankato, MN
012022

NOTE TO PARENTS AND EDUCATORS

Apex books are designed to build literacy skills in striving readers. Exciting, high-interest content attracts and holds readers' attention. The text is carefully leveled to allow students to achieve success quickly. Additional features, such as bolded glossary words for difficult terms, help build comprehension.

TABLE OF CONTENTS

CHAPTER 1
A WILD RIDE 5

CHAPTER 2
SKATEBOARD HISTORY 11

CHAPTER 3
SKATEBOARD STYLES 17

CHAPTER 4
SKATING TO WIN 23

Comprehension Questions • 28

Glossary • 30

To Learn More • 31

About the Author • 31

Index • 32

CHAPTER 1

A WILD RIDE

A skateboarder zooms off the edge of a **bowl** and into the air. He spins around twice. Then he glides back down the wall.

Skaters grab their skateboards in midair. That keeps boards from flying away during tricks.

An invert is also called a handplant.

6

Next, the skateboarder rolls up the bowl's other side. He plants his hand on the edge. His board and feet stick into the air.

Inverts are tricks where skateboarders flip upside down at the tops of ramps.

After that, the skateboarder jumps onto a rail and **grinds** down it. Then he leaps off to do even more tricks.

One common grind trick is the boardslide. The skater grinds the rail with the middle of the board.

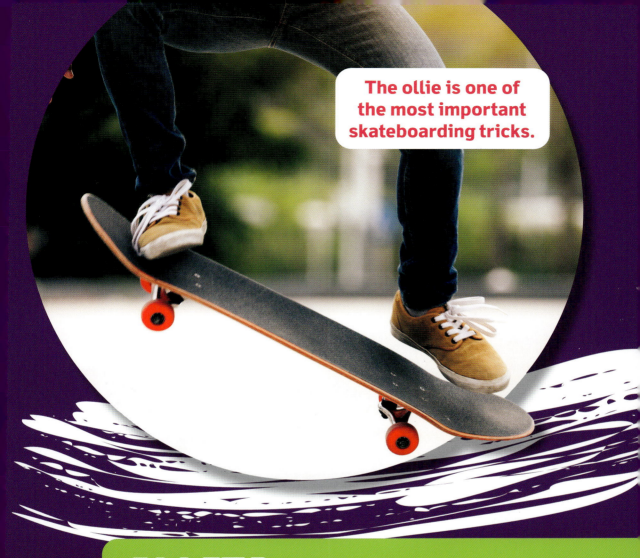

The ollie is one of the most important skateboarding tricks.

OLLIES

Skateboarders often use ollies to leap off the ground. In this move, one foot stomps down on the back of the skateboard. This sends the board and rider into the air.

CHAPTER 2

SKATEBOARD HISTORY

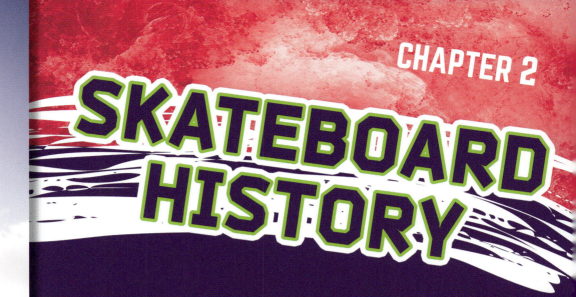

People began making skateboards in the 1900s. At first, they used metal wheels from roller skates. In the 1950s, designs improved. Clay wheels gave a smoother ride.

People still ride skateboards that are similar to the first kinds.

Some skateboards today have just one kicktail. They are often called cruisers.

In the 1970s, designs improved again. People made skateboards with plastic wheels. Boards got **kicktails**, too. These changes helped riders turn faster. They also helped riders do tricks.

SKATE PARKS

The first **skate park** opened in 1976. People go to skate parks to do tricks. They also learn skills from other skaters there.

Skate parks come in many shapes and sizes.

Skaters began competing against one another. The first X Games took place in 1995. These huge events made skateboarding well-known. Today, people skateboard all over the world.

In 2021, skateboarding was an Olympic sport for the first time. Skateboarders from 26 countries took part.

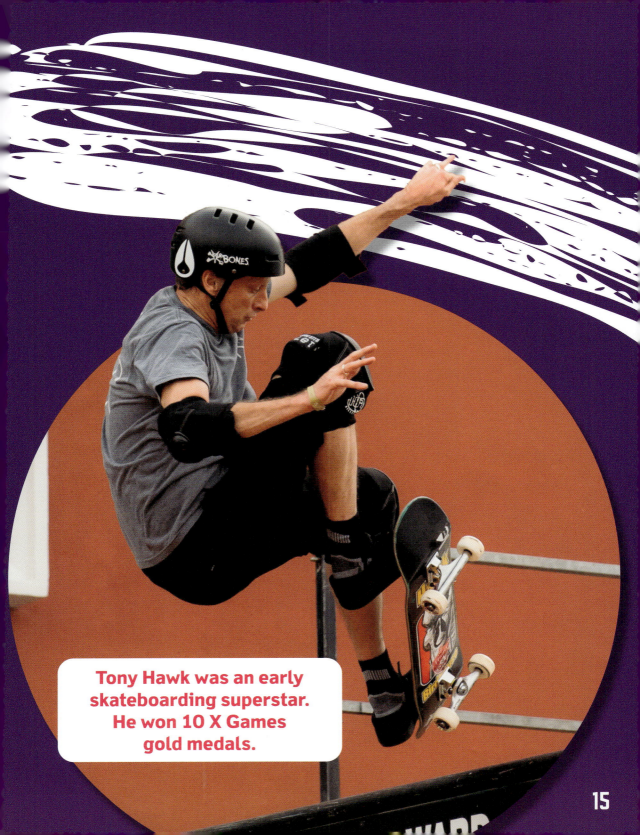

Tony Hawk was an early skateboarding superstar. He won 10 X Games gold medals.

CHAPTER 3
SKATEBOARD STYLES

Skateboarding has several styles. Park skateboarding takes place in a bowl. Skaters zoom up the walls. Then they do tricks in midair.

Park skateboarders often combine air tricks with grab tricks.

17

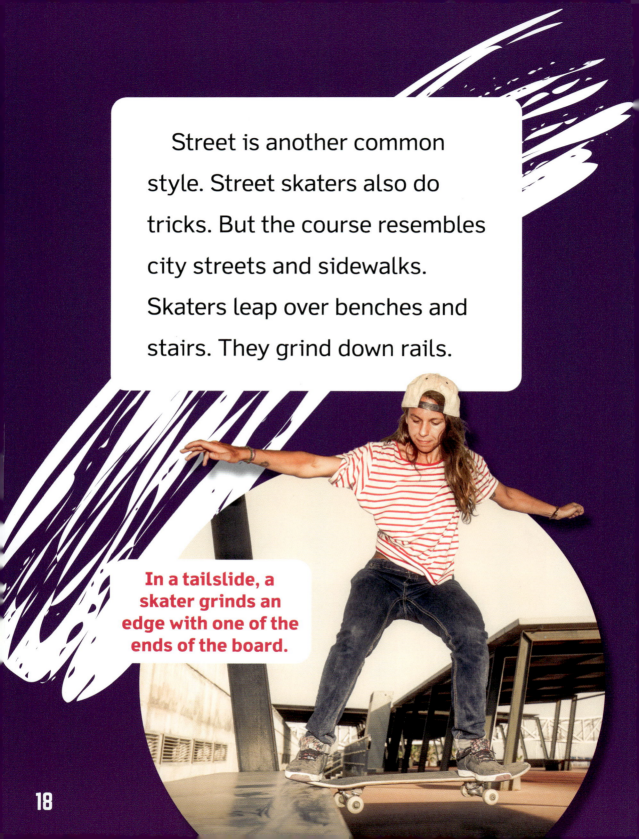

Street is another common style. Street skaters also do tricks. But the course resembles city streets and sidewalks. Skaters leap over benches and stairs. They grind down rails.

In a tailslide, a skater grinds an edge with one of the ends of the board.

Kickflips are common tricks in freestyle, street, and park skateboarding.

FREESTYLE

Freestyle is one of the oldest skateboarding styles. It happens on flat ground. Skaters do tricks. These tricks are often set to music.

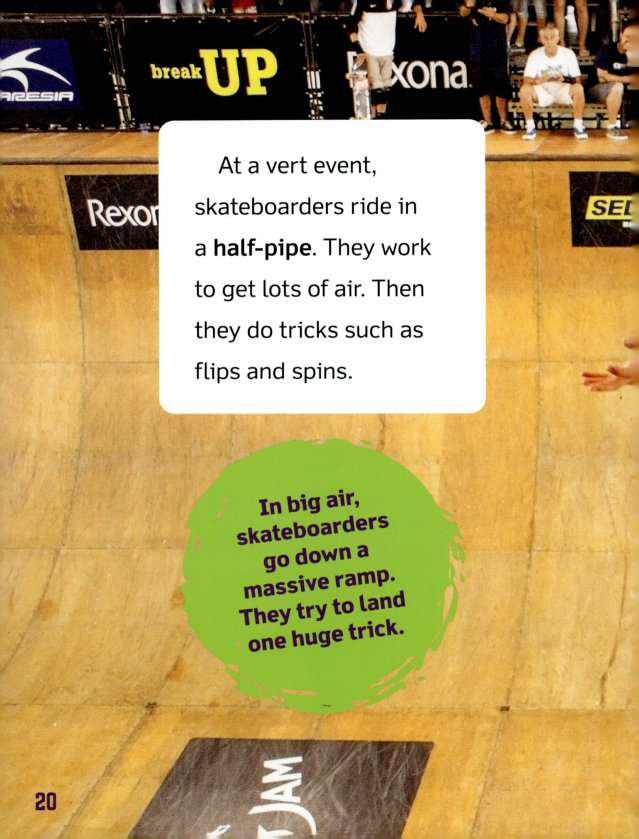

At a vert event, skateboarders ride in a **half-pipe**. They work to get lots of air. Then they do tricks such as flips and spins.

In big air, skateboarders go down a massive ramp. They try to land one huge trick.

Flips and spins are difficult skateboard tricks. The best skaters can flip and spin in the same trick.

CHAPTER 4
SKATING TO WIN

In skateboarding events, skaters get several **runs** to do tricks. Each run is usually 45 to 50 seconds long.

Skaters compete one at a time.

Judges watch skateboarders compete. They look for speed, flow, and **creativity**. Also, harder tricks get more points. Skaters' best runs are counted.

One hard trick is the frontside crooked grind. The skater grinds along the board's front trucks at an angle.

Many skaters try to land air tricks onto rails. Then they grind the rails to finish the tricks.

SHORTBOARDS

At events, most skaters use shortboards. This type of board has curves on its nose and tail. It also has narrower **trucks**. This shape helps skaters do tricks.

The top skaters advance to the next **round**. Skaters do more runs. Then the skater with the highest score wins.

In 2021, 13-year-old Rayssa Leal (left) of Brazil won Olympic silver for women's street skateboarding. Thirteen-year-old Momiji Nishiya (right) of Japan won gold.

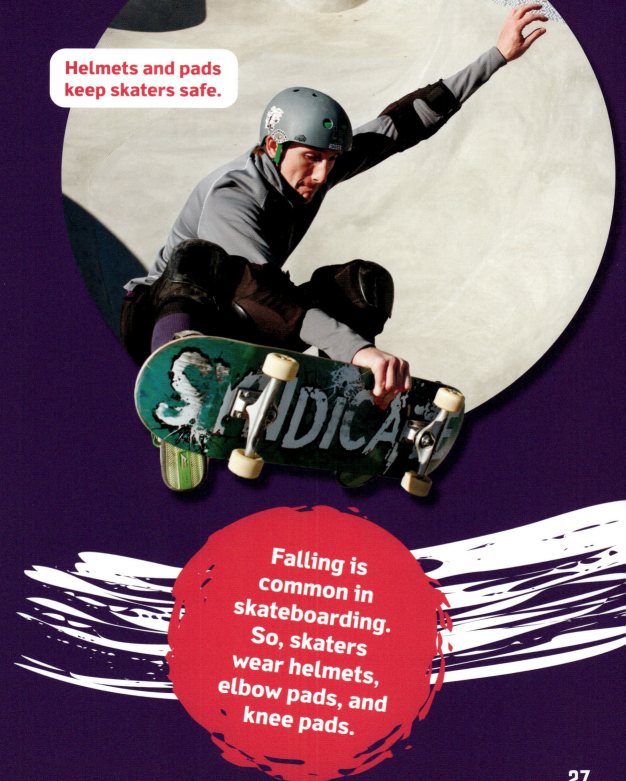

Helmets and pads keep skaters safe.

Falling is common in skateboarding. So, skaters wear helmets, elbow pads, and knee pads.

COMPREHENSION QUESTIONS

Write your answers on a separate piece of paper.

1. Write a paragraph summarizing the main ideas of Chapter 4.

2. Would you rather try street, park, or vert skateboarding? Why?

3. What material was used for the first skateboard wheels?

    A. clay
    B. plastic
    C. metal

4. Why do judges look at many parts of a skateboarder's run?

    A. Skating well is mostly based on luck.
    B. Skating well involves lots of different skills.
    C. There is only one way to skate well.

5. What does **resembles** mean in this book?

But the course resembles city streets and sidewalks. Skaters leap over benches and stairs.

    A. is similar to
    B. is different from
    C. is below

6. What does **massive** mean in this book?

In big air, skateboarders go down a massive ramp. They try to land one huge trick.

    A. easy to do
    B. short or small
    C. very tall or large

Answer key on page 32.

GLOSSARY

bowl
An area used for skateboarding that looks like an empty swimming pool with smooth walls.

creativity
Doing things in a way that is new or different.

grinds
Slides along a surface with part of a skateboard.

half-pipe
A U-shaped ramp that skateboarders go back and forth across.

kicktails
Curved ends of a skateboard.

round
One of several parts of a contest. Early rounds decide who moves on to the finals.

runs
In skateboarding, parts of a round. During a run, a skateboarder moves through a course and does tricks.

skate park
A place that has ramps, rails, and other structures where people can skateboard and do tricks.

trucks
Metal parts that connect the wheels to the skateboard.

TO LEARN MORE

BOOKS

Black, Christina. *Skateboarding*. Minneapolis: Abdo Publishing, 2021.

Kenney, Karen Latchana. *Extreme Skateboarding Challenges*. Minneapolis: Lerner Publications, 2021.

Lyon, Drew. *Downhill Skateboarding and Other Extreme Skateboarding*. North Mankato, MN: Capstone Press, 2020.

ONLINE RESOURCES

Visit **www.apexeditions.com** to find links and resources related to this title.

ABOUT THE AUTHOR

Bettie Boswell enjoys watching skateboarders at the park when picking up her granddaughter from school. Long ago, she tried to ride a skateboard that had metal wheels.

INDEX

B
big air, 20
bowls, 5, 7, 17

F
flips, 20
freestyle, 19

G
grinding, 8, 18

H
half-pipes, 20

I
inverts, 7

K
kicktails, 12

O
ollies, 9
Olympics, 14

P
park, 17

R
rails, 8, 18

S
shortboards, 25
skate parks, 13
spins, 5, 20
street, 18

V
vert, 20

W
wheels, 11–12

X
X Games, 14

Answer Key:
1. Answers will vary; **2.** Answers will vary; **3.** C; **4.** B; **5.** A; **6.** C